Not Sonnets
Observations from an Ordinary Life

Bonnie Thurston

Cinnamon Press
:: small miracles from distinctive voices ::

Published by Cinnamon Press
www.cinnamonpress.com

The right of Bonnie Thurston to be identified as author of this work has been asserted by her in accordance with the Copyright, Designs and Patent Act, 1988. © 2022, Bonnie Thurston.
ISBN 978-1-78864-128-9

British Library Cataloguing in Publication Data. A CIP record for this book can be obtained from the British Library.

All rights reserved. No part of this publication may be reproduced, stored in a retrieval system, or transmitted in any form or by any means, electronic, mechanical, photocopying, recording or otherwise without the prior written permission of the publishers. This book may not be lent, hired out, resold or otherwise disposed of by way of trade in any form of binding or cover other than that in which it is published, without the prior consent of the publishers.

Designed and typeset in Bodoni by Cinnamon Press. Cover design by Adam Craig © Adam Craig. From original artwork:Tree illustration 215273553 © Rodicabruma | Dreamstime,com

Cinnamon Press is represented by Inpress.

Acknowledgements

Some of the poems in this collection have previously appeared in books including ARTS 29/2, 2018. ('Evanescence'); *Andrew Blackmun, Holy One Go With Us,* Ring Lake Ranch, ('Receiving Place'); *From Darkness to Eastering,* Glasgow: Wild Goose Publications, 2017, www.ionabooks.com ('Returning').

And in these magazines: *Soul by Southwest,* ('Disguise'), *Spiritus,* ('This Gentler Way', 'Paramita') and *The Christian Century,* ('The Wrong Way Round', 'After the Storm', 'A Process not to be Hurried') as well as online at The Abbey of the Arts, ('*ad-din*').

Thanks to Cinnamon Press for publishing the book, and particularly to Jan for gentle and perceptive editing and to Adam for his glorious work on the cover.

Contents

Intuition ... 11

Home

Bring My Wastrel Heart Home ... 15
Receiving Place ... 16
Absent ... 17
Homeward ... 18
Returning ... 19
Explaining Home ... 20
Chimera ... 21
Belonging ... 22
Outside Time ... 23
The Wrong Way Round ... 24

Autumn

Autumnal Stillness ... 27
What Sustains ... 28
The Fallowness of Fall ... 29
Funeral Procession ... 30
Sticking Points ... 31
En Route to the Bus Stop ... 32
Paw-Paws ... 33

Winter

After the Storm ... 37
Winter Twilight ... 38
In Darkness ... 39
Insight ... 40
Evening: Deep Winter ... 41
Keep the Coals ... 42
Hibernation ... 43
Fear of Falling ... 44
Disguise ... 45
Ill Timed ... 46
Feeders ... 47
Solitary Snowdrop Blooming ... 48
Beware the Ides of March ... 49

Spring

A Process Not to be Hurried	53
Promissory	54
Forbidden Fruit	55
Spring	56
Church Parking Lot	57
Considering Seeds	58
Daffodils	59
Flash of Insight	60
Fire Eaters	61
Dame Julian of Norwich, May 8	62
Growing Things	63
This Gentler Way	64
Something Might Be	65

Summer

Different Orientation	69
Rose Garden	70
Evanescence	71
Gift of the Spirit	72
Convent Guest	73
Rainbows	74
Impenetrable	75
A Trick of the Light	76
No Flying Carpet	77
In Shadow	78
Garnering	79

Final Journey

ad-din	83
Siva	84
Late Life Hope	85
Role Reversal	86
Safety Patrol	87
Choice	88
In Life's Gloaming	89
Paramita	90

In memoriam: For my parents

Not Sonnets
Observations from an Ordinary Life

Intuition

Trust in perception
just at the edge
of consciousness,
knowingness
of a presence
neither malevolent
nor benign,
but there when
the heart's most
minute opening
turns toward it,
perceives obliquely
a facelessness
with the merest
hint of a smile.

Home

Bring My Wastrel Heart Home

To know
that always,
and everywhere,
the place
where I am,
where each stands,
is holy.

Holy is
not elsewhere.
There is
no elsewhere.
This is it.
We are it.
Attend.

Receiving Place

Place does not normally give
what one does not seek.
Receiving its gift
requires just being there,
listening into silence,
watching, waiting
like an osprey for fish,
like her chicks for supper,
like the thirsty sage
for evening's storm,
like great boulders
for lightning's shattering strike.
Knowing place requires
being broke open.

Absent

In the city
I feel absent from
the wedding feast,
its wet earth,
its growing things,
the secret life
which reveals itself
slowly, coquettishly
to those who wait.

I was invited early
to nature's nuptials,
know in green cathedrals,
skeletal winter hills,
the Bridegroom.

Homeward

for Margaret

I weary of the beauty
of steel and glass,
the glory of concrete,
the affluence of cities
where nations congregate.
My heart has turned
toward quietude,
the humbleness of home,
toward our river,
toward our mountains,
their sustaining solitudes
and majestic silences,
toward all that is small,
simple, longed for.

Returning

...in returning and rest ye shall be saved...

Isaiah 30:15b

Perhaps not immutable,
place is inexhaustible.
Returning to known ones
does not diminish them
or make them go dark,
but more luminous.
One sees what shines
through the surfaces,
notices more deeply details
that are the pulse of the place.
Returning, one migrates
from large to small,
attends to minuter things,
passes into place's infinity.

Explaining Home

Most people drive blindly by
on the crumbling state road
never seeing this house
perched precariously above it
where I hack back weeds,
trim encroaching trees
not yet dancing for joy
but on windy days trying.

In this extraordinarily
ordinary place I
put down deep roots
far from worldly paths
of power and plenty.
My star stopped here.

Chimera

I make my bed
every morning:
with old-fashioned
hospital corners,
a smoothed blanket.
Living alone,
this is unnecessary,
but a peculiar,
ancient ritual
that I enjoy,
beginning the day
with the illusion
of an ordered world,
so unlike its reality.

Belonging

I am an interested observer
along the ridge I drive
every Sunday morning.
Over years I've watched
a house sink into itself.
The yard went untended.
Then windows were broken.
Vines snaked ominously in.
The roof collapsed.
The walls soon followed.
Oddly, the process of decay
exuded the comfort of a truth:
Earth reclaims her own,
and I belong to earth.

Outside Time

Being outside time,
God is not experienced
by increments,
but suddenly
as a match struck
in a dark room
which proves to be
a treasure house,
as lightening bolts
explode the night sky
eclipse lesser, stellar light.
God is not temporal,
not process but Presence,
creation, infinite epiphany.

The Wrong Way Round

In a theological tome I read
opening the world to God
which echoes in my ear
a quarter tone off pitch,
just enough to make choirs
of angels and archangels wince.

Surely that is backwards.
The whole amazing universe,
every minute or enormous thing,
is a door opening into God,
a summons to eternity
in a dust-to-dust creation,
an invitation to adoration,
the substance of forever.

Autumn

Autumnal Stillness

I sometimes perceive
a palpable stillness
as if all earth's processes
pause for a moment
and are waiting.

I do not know
from whence
this quietness comes
or whether it goes anywhere.

I recognize it only
by the tiny stirring
of wonder
in the marrow
of my bones.

What Sustains

Extraordinary autumn's
late afternoon sun
turns the ground golden.
Bronze feathers illuminated,
a flock of wild turkeys
gleans in the stubble
of field corn recently
cut for cattle silage.

When something or
someone seems already
over, finished, what
sustains might still be
hidden in previously
harvested places.

The Fallowness of Fall

The life of the spirit is
never *one size fits all*,
never mass produced.
By natural processes,
a bespoke God
continues to craft
atoms and asters,
bacteria and biospheres,
chickens and children,
is resident, if hidden,
in individuated things.
However else could
the fallowness of fall be
the gestation of greening?

Funeral Procession

In places sophisticated people
think of as backwater,
we still respect the dead.
I stop at a crossroad
for the crocodile of cars
snaking toward the cemetery.
It gives me time to attend
to the feathery, rusty gray
of late autumn's forest,
contours of the leafless land.
The dying time of year
also deserves our respect
for the life that will arise
from its patient waiting.

Sticking Points

I had worked all morning
on an intractable problem,
a barrier to my project,
had searched the books,
taxed my addled brain,
scratched my empty head,
when close behind me
there was an ominous thud.
I turned to the window.
Two gray wisps of down,
feathery and wavering,
clung to the glass
where some other tiny life
had hit an invisible wall.

En Route to the Bus Stop

I was arrested by fallen leaves
on wet, black pavement,
the pattern of their pointedness,
the panoply of their yellows.
Attention to the daily and ordinary
offers invitation to reflection
on the noumenal and eternal,
reminds me that all created things,
and every earthly experience,
even an accustomed walk
to the bus on a rainy evening,
is a becoming toward whatever
is yet to be, whatever beckons
shyly from behind all that is.

Paw-Paws

for Marc

Like a pig snuffing truffles
I've been up on the hill
picking up paw-paws,
searching for them by smell:
sweet, slightly citrus,
Appalachia's tropical fruit,
for most an acquired taste.

Some years squashy under foot,
this year they're tooth-marked,
chewed, or already gone, which
signals a harsh winter coming.
The old folks like them black,
best, like so many things,
just before the rot sets in.

Winter

After the Storm

A morning of golden light
after two days' stormy darkness
illuminates the bleak twistedness
of trees now dressed, not in leaves,
but centuries' growth of lichens
and green, glowing mosses
that drape and devour their hosts.
After the orgy of wild wind dancing,
the limbs are quiet, as if awaiting
the giver of gale and gentleness.
They are like all the baptized
who arise from troubled waters
washed clean of all ugliness,
with one side still in darkness.

Winter Twilight

The temperature
dropped suddenly.
A slow, steady wind
blew minute snowflakes
in the frozen dusk,
tiny reminders
we all live
on the boundary
between light and dark,
between matter and air.
A chill in the bones
hisses, *you will die.*
And be healed, whispers
the rising evening star.

In Darkness

You cannot see them
on a moon-bright night
so illuminated and lovely
that dancing shadows
of winter waiting trees
make pleasing patterns
on ice-bejeweled snow.

Only in this unremitting
darkness could you glimpse,
widely scattered, far away,
translucent pearls of light,
a broken necklace longing
to be restrung, and yet,
like you, still luminous.

Insight

Winter and flu brought
a slowing and settling.
In gentle, friendly, forced,
and chosen solitude,
the silence of the house,
is peopled by the past
and unexpected gratitude.

It is like turning a page,
finding one's self in a new
chapter of a previously
incomprehensible book,
now read as compelling,
wonderfully insightful,
and completely good.

Evening: Deep Winter

Freezing rain became heavy snow.
Crystalline treasures of the garden
are cosseted as if in cotton wool.
Somewhere beneath the packing,
jewels await an appointed time.
I do not suffer winter's solitude,
prepare a seasoned roast
for the oven, pare sprouts.
If you were here, we'd have
wine with our meal, fragrant
with rosemary, and a glass
after as we'd sit companionably
reading into darkness
before the fire's crimson eye.

Keep the Coals

We were made for a lust
that requires regulating.
Smooring that fire isn't easy.
One hopes to keep the coals
without fanning the flames,
for if all fire dies out,
earth's wetness withers,
life itself is a drought,
a desert, a vast aridity
void of juice and joy,
fit only for the dust bin.
Keep kindling at ready,
but not bellows. Don't
blow on glowing embers.

Hibernation

As night grows colder, longer,
like other insignificant mammals
I seek warmth where it is found,
pull the pillow from the top,
the blanket from the bottom,
curl up in the bed's center
perhaps seeking to avoid
the tedium and rigor
of another ordinary day,
perhaps waiting for light,
for danger's darkness to pass,
perhaps hoping the heart
will again be strong enough
to leave its hibernation.

Fear of Falling

In emergent sun,
trees are polished
sterling silver.
Night rained ice,
then snowed
a white, downy,
virginal world

beneath which lurked
danger of falling,
being broken open
as the Cardinal's
daub of blood
on winter's
brittle branch.

Disguise

One arctic morning
at the year's dead end,
I was startled to see
on a frost-glazed branch
over an ice-covered creek,
a Kingfisher, crested, regal,
waiting for unwary prey,
or for watery winter sun
to irradiate his plumage,
or for me to recognize
with uncanny clarity
the avian disguise
of Christ, predisposed
to plunge, plunder, arise.

Ill Timed

Today, at absolutely
the wrong time of year
for their migration,
I saw a phalanx
of Canada geese
tearing across the sky
like ominous bombers
in WW II news reels.

Are they disordered,
lost, left behind
by their more timely,
better organized cohorts?

It is always, everywhere
the wrong time for bombers.

Feeders

Filling them alleviates
winter's contagion,
its monochrome cold,
its enfolding insularity
that threatens to freeze
the heart's concern
for others' suffering.

On this frigid landscape,
the emptiness of snow,
a flutter of wings descends
seeking hope in fallen seed.
Sufficient unto today,
tomorrow's promise is
unfulfilled, but anticipated.

Solitary Snowdrop Blooming

We endured an arctic freeze.
Now, mounded snow
melts in welcome sun.
For reasons unintelligible,
an unexpected, unseasonable
reprieve is reminiscent
of the piety of unbelievers
who suddenly pray
in danger, on deathbed,
find themselves helped,
healed, delivered,
stupefied, as surprised
as this solitary Snowdrop
blooming in winter.

Beware the Ides of March

In lovely foretaste of future,
temperatures soared skyward.
Peachy dawn promised bright days.
Returned birds sang avian duets.
Two robins intently engaged
in awkward, complex sex dance.

But today is shrouded in frost
and winter's watery light.
Three does in winter coats
limp across the icy hill
nibbling at what there is to eat,
bark on the young pear trees
that will not blossom
when spring finally arrives.

Spring

A Process Not to be Hurried

Long solitude is a gradual
drawing inward, going deeper,
like autumn planted bulbs
snuggling into the soil,
marinating in darkness
to flower forth in spring.

When the isolation ends
and blossoming is invited,
do not hurry the process.
First the shy, green shoot,
then the tentative tip
of a fragile stalk arises
to carry a bud opening
slowly, in its own time.

Promissory

In early March
buds begin to swell
on my peach tree.
It is too soon.
This uncertain month
delivers snow and frost
with warm, sweet winds.

But there they are,
small, swelling promises
of succulent fruit,
nature's resurrective *fiat*
silently shouting down
my winter worry
with summer certainty.

Forbidden Fruit

A Goldfinch still dressed
in his olive winter coat
first flew into the window
beyond which the longed for
lush green of house plants
tantalizingly beckoned.
Does his avian brain
know them not mirage?
Now, he perches on the sill,
pecks gently at the pane,
head slightly cocked
at a quizzical angle,
knowing what is there,
not why it is forbidden.

Spring

Ruffling his feathers,
and having them ruffled
by a wind still wintery,
a dusty sparrow perches
on a sunny window sill,
warbles for the joy of it,
then flutters up one story,
lands on an air conditioner
from behind which a small,
demure female sparrow
emerges and ignores him,
as the eternal drama
of he and she unfolds
before my bemused eyes.

Church Parking Lot

Not one for handshakes and gossip,
I slipped out before the last hymn,
at the edge of the parking lot
met eye-to-eye a grizzly-muzzled
old brown hunting dog hunkered
in the bed of a black pick up.
I was beneath notice as he waited
patiently for his foolish human
wasting a splendid spring morning
better spent marking territory,
sniffing out who else was around,
chasing rabbits, treeing squirrels,
being completely, gloriously
exactly what God made him.

Considering Seeds

I park my battered Subaru
amidst the pick-up trucks,
now stand gaping at racks
of envelopes of seeds
each with a colorful picture
of a perfect vegetable
which I never achieve.
I want to plant them all,
strive to be realistic about
my tiny plot's possibilities.
It is a cold, late April
with frost most mornings,
far too early to plant,
never too early to hope.

Daffodils

My house is encircled
by cheerful flowers,
fruit of the bulbs
planted by hundreds
every autumn
for thirty years.
Old folks call them
Lenten Lilies; they
are gone by Easter.
Trumpeting spring, they
show the external face
of a modest bungalow,
a happy visage without
hint of darkness within.

Flash of Insight

Bearing others' suffering
brings undertones of fire
in the silence of night.
I live a fragile balance
of intellect and intuition,
know, often piercingly,
but not how I know.

I fear being an ember,
Easter's explosive
bright, crimson flash
followed by Lenten
smear of dead ash.
We give light in darkness
by being consumed.

Fire Eaters

The fire-eaters consume
great burning torches
that, swallowed unflinchingly,
go down the little red hatch.
For most ordinary mortals
combustion is a spark within,
smoored like a hearth fire
that requires finding, fanning,
being carefully blown upon
by the breath of one's own life
to become a conflagration
in which self is immolated,
leaves only perfumed embers,
but lights another's way.

Dame Julian of Norwich, May 8

After late frost,
desperate drooping
in a flowered garden
is followed by brilliance
of the morning sun
on a white wall,
oddly, seen only
in peripheral vision,
but all gentle reminders
that life's difficulties,
and they are legion,
even imperfectly glimpsed
might be shy unveilings
of Love's shining face.

Growing Things

After a warm late April
a chilly middle May.
The trees don't leaf out,
slow the hills' greening.
Seeds planted too early
refuse to germinate.

Nothing and no one
blossoms and flourishes
when the soil is cold,
the sun withdraws
behind indifferent clouds,
the life-giving water
of ordinary kindness is
withheld, withdrawn, absent.

This Gentler Way

I am enamored
of early morning's
slow dawning, which
reveals things obscured
by day's full brightness.
The gradual appearance
of shadowy things
about self and others
which, in harsher light,
might involve judgment,
illumined this gentler way,
evokes understanding,
mercy's back-door that
might open into love.

Something Might Be

National Public Radio's
announcer said that astronomers
think the thrumming in space
might be left over bits
of electromagnetic energy.
Something is certainly
pulsing through the universe.

It might, in fact, be pulsars.
But it might be something else,
something entirely different,
something less impassive,
say, an enormous infusion
of incorporeal, pervasive,
and promiscuous love.

Summer

Different Orientation

I listen in early morning
to that gentlest of sounds,
a quiet summer rain.
It brings invitation
to green things to grow,
offers the possibility
of a different orientation,
to receive what is given,
to enter the seed's mystery
which grows as it will,
content to wait in earth
for heaven's summons
which might be heard,
in the dawn-bird's warble.

Rose Garden

I spend the summer afternoon
in aimless meandering
through ranks of roses
of every imaginable color.
Like the bees, I drink
their intoxicating attar.
Then, in a shaded arbor,
one small, yellow blossom,
each petal perfectly formed
and all opening in consort,
quietly, perceptively whispers,
In a barbarous world, beauty
is not luxury, but necessity
and always individuated.

Evanescence

for Cheryl

The most real things
are not substantial,
knowing oneself loved;
hearing the rarest word
a glittering truth.
Think of real things,
fidelity, faith, freedom.
Consider a perfect rose.
Its velvety petals will
fall in tonight's rain
that will wash dawn.
Beauty is intangible,
its evanescence enduring
joy and, perhaps, enough.

Gift of the Spirit

for Esther

Some have been given
a gift of hospitality
not only of home
but of heart,
a quality of welcome
for the weary,
acceptance of what
the bearer brings,
a balm for life's bruises
that arises only when
a host has been healed
of life's slings and arrows,
who, broken and giving,
can abundantly bless.

Convent Guest

Always, some of the nuns
are genuinely welcoming.
Others crucify with their eyes.
It is a dangerous business
to open your home,
to open your heart
to wandering strangers.
You might be mistaken
or taken advantage of.
But then again some have
entertained angels unaware.
That odd little Nazarene
or his friends might arrive,
take up permanent residence.

Rainbows

In the convent's comfortable austerity
flowers provide feasts for the eye,
perishable jewels carefully arranged
to enrich undecorated lives,
to give glory to a God
whose gratuity is evidenced
by color life does not require.
We would survive in black and white,
but God recycles rays
of decomposed light,
declares with Divine exuberance,
Let there be rainbows!

Impenetrable

For weeks a song sparrow
has flung itself against
the sitting room window,
repeatedly thumped against
that unseen barrier
to its unknown desire,
then perched on a branch,
lifted its befuddled head,
warbled celestial sweetness.
Nothing I have devised
discourages this obsession,
this small, avian breakdown,
or perhaps something else,
something also impenetrable.

A Trick of the Light

Late afternoon sun
on a sycamore tree
creates an artist's study
in shades of green.
The layered texture of leaves
quivers in a faint breeze
or perhaps a gentle breath.
Once again I sense
that something more real
stands behind this world,
which is animate with it,
offers constant invitation
to love what is here
for the sake of that other.

No Flying Carpet

In authentic oriental rugs
there is always a flaw,
a break in the intricate pattern.
The women who weave them
know that God alone is perfect.
Their carpets are not for flying
to heaven's fountained paradise,
but for earth's hungry eyes,
the sore feet of desert wanderers.
They are jewel-toned reminders
that imperfection roots us
in this beautiful, broken world,
tempers our temptation
to long for the little not given.

In Shadow

...we see Him at best only in shadows...

St. John Henry Newman

Truth. Yet the unspoken fact is the
benevolence to envisage Him
only in the safety of shadow,
a shade in peripheral vision
whom we glimpse only as passing light,
as filtered by the trees' summer leaves,
or the edge of dreams upon waking
with bits remembered and forgotten.

No one sees Him straight on and survives.
The splendor of His Light is too bright.
Its pure perfection would vaporize
or blind us to created beauty,
engender insatiable hungers
for which one ever thereafter longs.

Garnering

Crops are planted
in long ribbons
around the hills,
unfurl brown, green,
fallow, furrowed,
or fecund.
Wide swaths
of knee-high corn
undulate under
the wind's hand,
like all things,
move inexorably
toward inevitable harvest.

Final Journey

ad-din

Beneath the forms,
the eternal essence,
multitudinous variations
reflecting Divine kindness:
the gift of many ways
for many peoples,
all beloved, all desired.

When the wind blows,
grasses of the fields
bow down in ranks.
Flowers are multiform,
but all yearn toward
a singular source of light:
the Face behind the faces.

ad-din is 'quintessential religion'.

Siva

God dances in a halo of fire,
whirls through a universe
spinning around that dance.
Incendiary music is pitched
too high for human hearing,
but its insistent rhythm
pulses through our veins.
God's steps are too intricate
for our faltering clay feet,
but their beauty calls us
to stumble toward them,
to raise our sullied hands
and make of our fingers
fire to light the way.

Late Life Hope

Moving into life's winter,
I watch companions
of youth and middle age
begin to drop away
like autumn's slow demise.
The flowers finish,
bow heads, drop blossoms.
According to their natures,
trees turn rusty or bright.
Daylight dims; darkness deepens
as forests become skeletal.
Surely the roots go deeper,
draw sustenance from sources
mysterious and unknown.

Role Reversal

You realize those you admired,
the women you wanted to be
when you grew up, are all gone,
have crossed the threshold into
whatever service comes next
for role models of compassion.
Nobody is ahead of you in line.
Your heart lurches wildly,
knowing you are the grown up.
Nobody consoles or comforts you,
puts plasters on your brokenness.
Just as it once was for them,
this lonely and terrifying task
is now yours to do for others.

Safety Patrol

Even the wayward world
can settle into peace, palpable
for those willing to stop,
to look, to listen toward
the last, inevitable reality:
the great street crossing.

Life is a dangerous place.
Caution is necessary.
But there is a beauty
that points beyond itself
to its shadowy source,
the space where one is found,
that prescription for safety
in life's dangerous crossings.

Choice

To bring them healing, Moses
put a bronze snake on a pole,
forced the people to gaze
on the horror that bit them.
Christ, Himself, preferred
the cup to pass him by, but
drank it to the bitter dregs.
To make the torment disappear
one old desert monk thrust
his head in the demon's mouth.
Not by evasion, but choosing
the thing most feared
move through it into freedom,
move through it into life.

In Life's Gloaming

O Evening, you bring home all that bright dawn has scattered...

Sappho, Evening Star

Cows, of conscience, come home.
Chickens, of confusion, roost.
The hard edges of things fade.
Light lengthens, wanes in the west.
Songs of small birds modulate
toward the owl's ominous hoot.
Creatures of the night creep
about their nocturnal business.
The wise lessen the urge to assert.
Kindness overcomes judgment.
Tolerance ascends the heart's throne.
And we go to our rest in peace,
lay down, awaiting with assurance
the dawn of the new day.

Paramita

No passport is required
to reach that shore.
For some, the crossing
requires long journey.
For most it means
waking up to their
who, where, when.
We cannot travel
to where we are.
We do not create
what already is,
but can recognize
its incendiary beauty,
know we are there.

www.ingramcontent.com/pod-product-compliance
Lightning Source LLC
LaVergne TN
LVHW041306080426
835510LV00009B/874